The Real Magnet Book

by MAE FREEMAN

Pictures by NORMAN BRIDWELL

SCHOLASTIC BOOK SERVICES

NEW YORK • TORONTO • LONDON • AUCKLAND • SYDNEY • TOKYO

Text copyright © 1967 by Mae Freeman. Illustrations copyright © 1967 by Norman Bridwell. All rights reserved. Published by Scholastic Book Services, a division of Scholastic Magazines, Inc.

8th printing .... March 1974

Printed in the U.S.A.

The
Real
Magnet
Book

A Magnet Can Pull Things

There is a little metal bar taped to the last page of this book. Peel off the tape. Pick up the bar and look it over carefully. There does not seem to be anything unusual about it. It looks like any old piece of metal. If you saw it in the street, you might not even stop to pick it up.

But the bar you are holding is really quite special. It is a **magnet**, and it has the power to pull certain things. You can do some science experiments to test the pulling power of your magnet.

Get a paper clip and lay it on the table.

Then push your magnet slowly along the table, closer and closer to the clip. Suddenly, the clip will snap over to the magnet and stick there. It seems almost as if an invisible rubber band pulled the clip to the magnet.

Try the experiment again and again.

Watch closely.

You will be able to see a little space between the magnet and the clip, just before they snap together. This shows that the pulling power of the magnet works even before the magnet and the clip touch.

The Shapes of Magnets

A magnet does not have to be a straight
bar, like yours.

There are

magnets shaped like a horseshoe

magnets shaped like a U

magnets shaped like a cake

magnets shaped like a ring

and other shapes, too.

The Pulling Power of a Magnet Comes from Atoms

Why do magnets have this wonderful pulling power? Scientists have found out why. They know that everything in the world is made of little specks called **atoms**. Atoms are so small that you cannot see them, even with the strongest microscope. In this little dot · there are *billions and billions* of atoms.

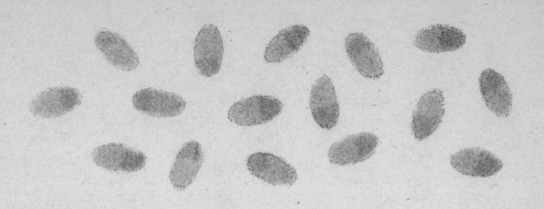

Some atoms face up, and some face down. Some face one side, and some face another. Atoms face every way, helter-skelter.

Most magnets are made of iron, and iron atoms are very special. Each one has a tiny, tiny bit of pulling power. Usually, the atoms in a piece of iron are all jumbled, and their pulling power does not show up.

But there are ways of turning iron atoms to make them face the same way. Then all the little bits of pulling power can work together. That is how a piece of iron becomes a magnet that can pull other pieces of iron.

When your magnet was made, the atoms in it were turned so that they face one way. The metal of your magnet is extra hard, so the atoms are not able to turn helter-skelter again. Your magnet will *stay* a magnet. It is a *permanent* magnet.

So far, your magnet has pulled only a clip. Paper clips are made with iron. Now test the pulling power of your magnet on other kinds of things.

Here is a list.

Does the magnet pull it?
Put an X under the right answer.
Yes   No

rubber ball

tin can

a dime

spool of thread

bottle cap

teacup

steel wool

You can see from your answers that a magnet pulls some kinds of things but not others. It pulls only the things that have iron in them.

Put a small piece of paper on top of the clip. Bring the magnet slowly down to the paper, right over the clip.

The clip will be pulled up along with the paper. This experiment proves that the pulling power of a magnet works through paper.

Next, put a piece of aluminum foil over the clip and do the experiment.

Try it also with a piece
of cloth over the clip.

Each time, the clip will snap
to the magnet. The pulling
power of a magnet works
through many things.

Magnet Mystery Boat

You did an experiment to show that the pulling power of a magnet works through paper, aluminum, and cloth. The pulling power works through some other things, too.

Make a mystery boat to show how the pulling power of a magnet works through glass and through water.

Get five tacks

and a cork from a bottle.

Push the tacks into the cork in a straight row along the side. Stick each tack all the way in, so only the head shows.

Cut a small piece of paper in the shape of a sail, and put a pin through it. Turn the cork so the row of tacks is at the bottom. Stick the pin and sail into the top.

Put some water into a glass pie plate. There should be just enough water to make your boat float.

Set the pie plate up on two boxes. Do not set it on cans or on anything else that may have iron in it.

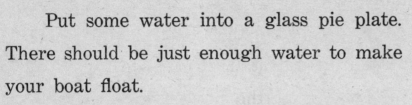

Carefully put your sailboat into the water. If the boat rolls over, stick the pin into a new place on the cork. The boat will balance when the pin is straight up and the tacks are at the bottom.

Hold your magnet against the under-side of the pie plate, near the boat. Now, when you move the magnet, the boat will move too. The magnet pulls the iron tacks in the boat. The pulling power of the magnet works right through the glass and the water.

Try another way of sailing the boat. Hold the magnet in the air, close to the front of the boat.

The boat will slowly follow the magnet, even though the magnet does not touch the cork or the tacks.

If the boat gets too near the side of the plate, it may stick there. Put the boat back into the middle of the plate. Then you can move it again with your magnet.

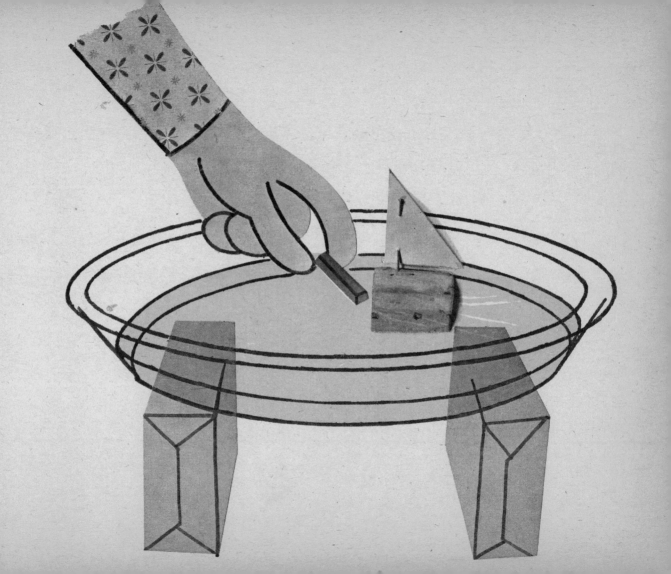

Magnet Fishing Pole

If you put anything made of iron near a magnet, it can become a magnet too. You can see this happen if you make a magnet fishing pole.

Get:

a drinking glass

a piece of string

a pencil

some sugar

some very small tacks

Put the tacks into the glass.

Sprinkle sugar on the tacks until they are just covered. It should look as if there is nothing but sugar in the glass.

Tie one end of the string around the middle of your magnet. Tie the other end to the top of the pencil. This will be your magnet fishing pole.

Hold the pole over the glass and let the magnet rest on the sugar. Then slowly lift the fishing pole, and the magnet will bring some tacks up with it. Watch them come up through the white sugar almost like magic.

Most of the tacks bunch up around the ends of the magnet. Sometimes they hang in loops or chains from one end of the magnet to the other. This is because a magnet is strongest at its two ends.

Notice that some of the tacks do not touch the magnet itself. They are pulled out of the sugar because they stick to other tacks. The iron tacks become magnets while they are near your permanent magnet.

You can go fishing again and again until you think there are no more tacks hidden in the sugar. But then — touch the magnet all over the top of the sugar. You might bring up one last little tack that you missed before.

When you finish fishing with your magnet, be sure to throw the sugar away. Save the tacks for other experiments.

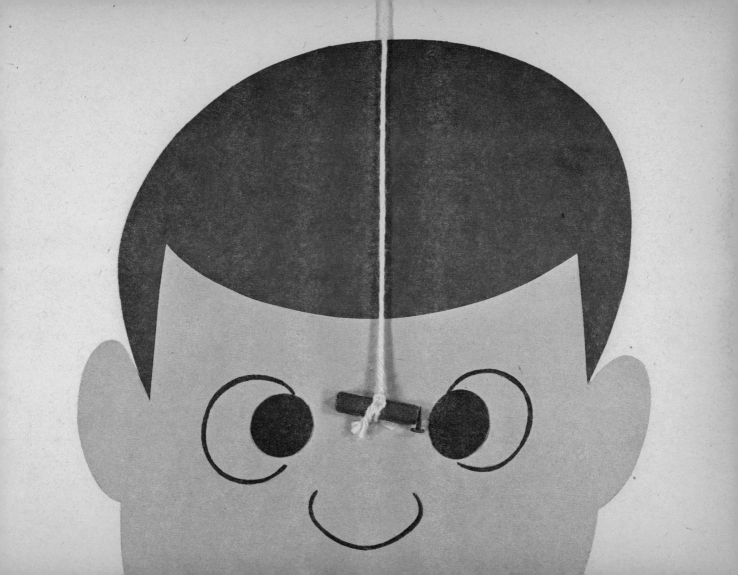

The Hanging Magnet

The two ends of a magnet look exactly alike, but they are really different in some ways. Do an experiment to find out how the ends of your magnet are different.

Tie one end of a piece of string tightly around the middle of your magnet. Tape the other end to the edge of a chair. The magnet should hang near the floor.

Slide the knot of the string back and forth until you find the place where the magnet balances.

The next thing to do is to ask someone
to point toward the north.

Now look at your hanging magnet, and
you will see that one end of it is also pointing
toward the north.

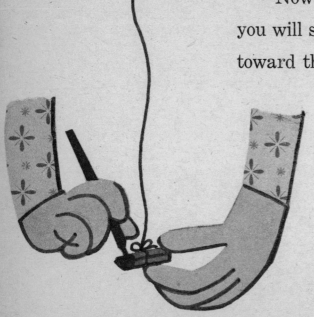

Use a felt marking pen to color
the north end of the magnet.

Now give the magnet a little twist and let go. When the magnet stops turning, you will see that the end with the color is pointing north again.

Every magnet has a north end and a south end. That is how the two ends of a magnet are different from each other.

Use Your Magnet to Make a Compass

You can use your hanging magnet as a **compass**. A compass is a pointer that shows how to find the north, wherever you are.

Get a piece of paper and draw a circle on it. You can make a good circle if you put a drinking glass on the paper and draw around the edge.

Print an N for north at the top of the circle.

Print an S for south at the bottom of the circle.

Print an E for east at the right side of the circle.

Print a W for west at the left side of the circle.

Put the paper on the floor under the magnet. Turn the paper so that the north end of the magnet points to the N. Then the other letters on the paper will tell you how to find south, east, and west, too.

You can use your compass indoors or outdoors. The end of the magnet with the color on it will turn to point north.

There is one thing to watch out for. Be sure there is no iron nearby to swing the magnet aside.

Use Your Magnet to Make a Magnet

You can make a magnet out of any piece of iron. Make one out of a darning needle. Needles are made of steel, and steel is a hard kind of iron.

Rub one end of your bar magnet gently along the needle from the head to the sharp end. Then start back near the head of the needle and rub again. Be sure not to turn the magnet in your fingers. The pictures show exactly how to do the rubbing.

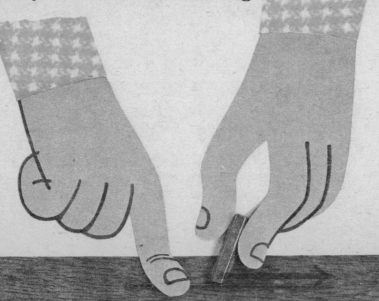

Make 25 rubs along the needle, always from the head to the sharp end. When you do this, you are making the atoms face the same way. That is what makes the needle a magnet.

Prove that your needle is now a magnet. Put a paper clip on the table and touch it with either end of the needle. As you slowly lift the needle, it pulls the clip up with it.

Magnets Can Pull
and Magnets Can Push

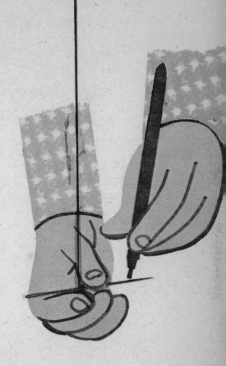

Use your needle magnet to find out something new that magnets can do.

First, tie a thread around the needle and hang it from a chair, just as you did when you made a compass. Make a mark on the end of the needle that points north. The other end is the south end.

On this needle, the sharp end is the one that points north.

Now set a large drinking glass on the floor so the needle hangs inside it. Wait until the needle stops turning.

Then, with the *north* end of your bar magnet, touch the glass just at one side of the south end of the needle. The south end turns to meet your magnet. The glass keeps the needle from sticking to the magnet.

Take your magnet away from the glass, and wait until the needle stops swinging. Then touch the glass at the very same place with the *south* end of your magnet. This time, the needle turns away.

With the *south* end of your magnet, touch the glass just at one side of the *north* end of the needle. Watch the north end of the needle swing around to meet the south end of your magnet.

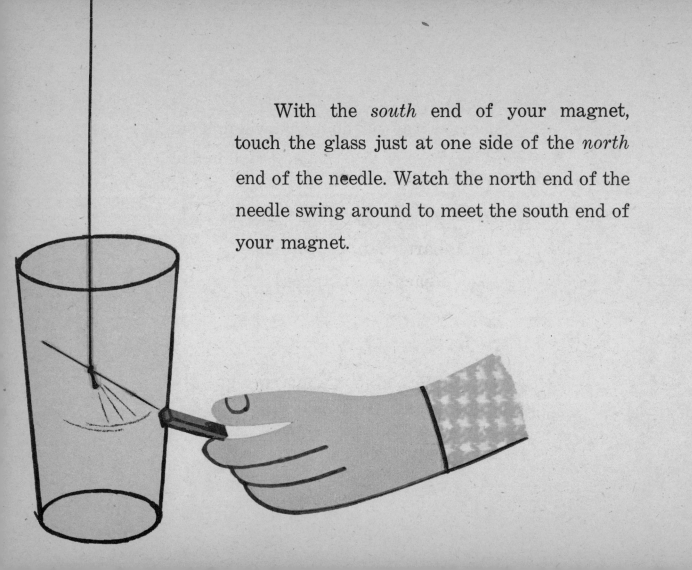

Whichever way you do it, you will find out two very important things about magnets:

1. The north ends of two magnets push each other apart. The south ends of two magnets push each other apart.

BUT

2. The north end of one magnet and the south end of the other magnet pull together.

There is another way to do a push-and-pull magnet experiment. You will need two bar magnets, so borrow another one from a friend. Then hang it by a thread so you can find the north end. Mark the north end and then take the thread off.

Hold one magnet in each hand. The *north ends* of the magnets should face each other. Move them slowly toward each other and try to make them meet.

Hold them tightly! They will push aside and almost wiggle out of your hands. It will be hard to make them touch!

Turn both magnets around so the *south ends* face each other. You will feel the same wiggling and pushing away.

Now try the experiment once more. But this time do it with the *north end* of one magnet facing the *south end* of the other. This time, they will snap together!

Now you have proved once more that—

1. The ends of two magnets push apart if they are the same.

2. The ends of two magnets pull together if they are different.

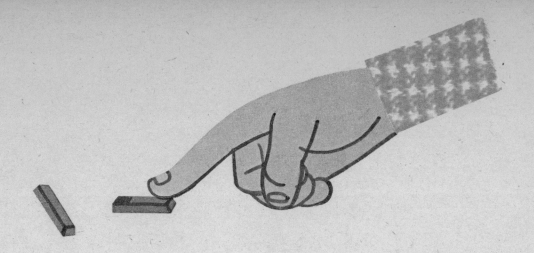

Put one of your bar magnets on a smooth table. Slide the other magnet slowly along the table, with one end pointing toward the first magnet. Suddenly the first magnet swings around to meet the magnet in your hand.

Which end of the magnet swings around? You can figure out the answer to this question even before you try the experiment. Just remember what happened in your other push-and-pull experiments.

Making an Electromagnet

You made a magnet out of a needle All you had to do was to rub the needle with your magnet in a special way.

Now make a magnet in a different way, by using electricity.

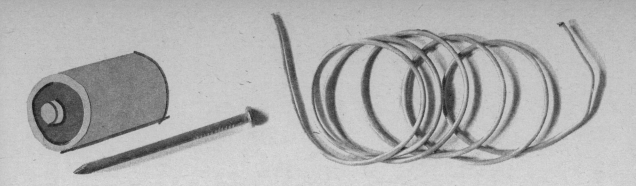

Get the biggest nail you can find. You
will also need a piece of bell wire and a dry-
cell battery from a flashlight.

Scrape the covering off each end of the
wire. Then wind the wire about 25 times
around the nail, over and over, as the picture
shows.

Notice that there is a little round button on top of the battery. The bottom of the battery is flat. Tape one end of the wire tight to the flat bottom of the battery.

Put a little pile of tacks on the table. Pick up the loose end of the wire and hold it down on the button. Then ask a friend to put the point of the nail into the pile of tacks and lift it slowly away. A bunch of tacks comes up with the nail.

While the tacks hang on the magnet, lift the wire off the battery button. The tacks drop back to the table.

The work of a battery is to keep electricity moving through the wire. When the wire touches the button, the electricity goes around and around the nail, and makes it a magnet.

When the wire is off the button, the electricity cannot get through. Then the nail is not a magnet any more.

A magnet made in this way by electricity is called an **electromagnet**. It is useful because it has pulling power that can be turned on and off.

There are huge electromagnets that work just like the one you made. The wires go around and around inside a thick iron box shaped like a cake.

When the electricity is turned on, the iron becomes a strong magnet. Then it can lift things even as heavy as automobiles.

There are electromagnets in many things that you use every day. There are electromagnets in your telephone, doorbell, refrigerator, automobile. There are huge electromagnets in railroad trains, ships, power stations, atom smashers.